The Hoopoe's Eye

Mark Carson

for Jane
who shared it all

and to
Paco, Francisco and Ricardo
who helped so much

Monday 22 October 2018

Buenas tardes Jane

Siento comunicarle que el río ha entrado
ayer por la tarde en su casa, mucho más que
la última vez. A 2 metros de altura aproxi-
madamente...
Tambien se ha llevado el puente sobre el
río y el puente nuevo de la Cueva del Gato...

Good evening Jane
I'm sorry to tell you that the river has entered
your house yesterday evening, much more than
the last time. 2 metres depth approximately...

Also it has carried away the bridge over the river
and the new bridge of the Cueva del Gato...

The New Footbridge

It springs across the river like a slice of rainbow,
arched as a vertebrate, golden in the sunlight
and the mayor cuts the ribbon, the councillors are ready
and they all march together, march across the Guadiaro.

Is it not a great idea, a bridge so light and springy?
the laminated timbers so pretty and so buoyant?
The abutments are substantial, the footings thick and massive
and the bridge rests lightly, lightly on its ledges.

*   *   *

The rain fell heavy in the Guadiaro catchment,
red with mud the river rose, covering the footings
and the river surged and rose again, thrusting the abutments
and again the turbid river rose, tearing at the handrails.

Who could imagine the buoyancy of timber?
Who would consider the drag loads on the structure?
Who did the sums on the piddling little brackets,
the tension, the shear, the bending and the torsion?

The goats and the sheep retreated to the hilltops,
watched as the racing spate tore the banks asunder,
watched as the carcasses were tumbled down the valley,
watched as the pretty footbridge wrenched itself to pieces.

Where will it end, the bridge, and what the hell can stop it?
Smashing through the gorges, crunching on the boulders,
tossing under viaducts and swept across the weir,
the stepping stones, past long-abandoned piggeries

until it crashes, snags against the Old Bridge.
Snags and floats and traps the trunks of willow trees,
of splintered fractured alamos and olive brash and figs
and oleander torn from sodden banks. It rises like a floating dam,

the water flooding over terraces, creeping up the door frames,
sluicing through the sockets and the fusebox, lifting tables
chairs cupboards sofas floating in a tangle to the ceiling,
twisting shutters from their pintle hinges, toilet doors,

unhanging pictures, prints. Guitars from hooks. Cushions.
Books from shelves, maps and guides from folders,
useless telephone directories, magazines
a grim confetti, paper-porridge slopping in the slimy flow.

There's no transparency, just thick brown oxtail
rich in clay washed from the groves of olives,
ploughed lands, hillsides scarified and naked.
Quietly it starts to settle, thick and smeary.

Now the water's reached the Old Bridge deck,
crushing foliage up against the chainlink handrail.
Abruptly the bridge gives way, the concrete pier
collapses, prising its footing from the river bed.

A hundred thousand tonnes of water make a charge for freedom
down the valley, tearing the gable from the house below,
scattering roof tiles. From the broken windows
of the flooded houses water spews.

Nothing prepares you

for the gap-toothed river bank
the fig tree swept aside
the quince trees piled
on top of the pear

    nor for the windows swinging
    loose behind their grilles
    the shutters gone
    turning the house to a hovel

nor for the garden shed
the tools canes poles
piled like spillikins
the buckets slopping over

    nor for the terraces
    smothered in sludge
    and the sausage factory's
    grease excretions.

Push on the doors
they're jammed
with god knows what
tumbled behind.

    You're forced to force
    an entrance.
    Something gives,
    something cracks.

Riverside Picnic

Sun's out. Mud's everywhere.
The rattan armchair's plastered over,
wattle-and-daub. In once-white filthy
coveralls, we can sit anywhere.

Lean back. Peel ham
(1 euro pack) scrunch it
on multigrain into a mouthful.
Suck juice from a box.

Now, there flutters by
a sulphur-yellow butterfly.
A heron makes his pass
down-river, purposefully.

Across the wall, two lads
are heaving shovels heaped
with muck from pool to barrow
high above their heads.

Why can't I do that?
Why'm I not twenty-three,
fit and muscled
like a matador?

Later they come across,
help us shift furniture,
get stuck in. Shovel
and shovel. Bravo amigos!

Vagrant

Chumff, chumff, two straight-edge shovels scrape across the floor,
you want to say, watch out for the tiles, but the job
will last forever if you interfere. Then there's the shout;

ancient, heavy-bodied, patterned-like-a-turkish-carpet,
A Gecko! they cry and lift him tenderly on the spade's tip,
carry him over to the light. A Patriarch of Thousands.

Off he trots, into the next day, the next year,
across the car park, back to the river
which only last week dropped him off.

Discobolus Technique

Form a scoop with your paw,
       pretend you're a bear
who scoops out ice-cream
       from a bucket; coffee or chocolate?

Freezing, it slips on your skin,
       extrudes through your fingers
like pottery clay. Resist the temptation
       to lick. It smells faintly awful.

You are doing this because
       the ice cream/clay is stuck in the bucket.
Dig it out with a spoon,
       it sticks to the spoon.
Scrape the spoon with a trowel,
       it sticks to them both.

So swing your fat clayball
       under-arm, hurl it backhand
with a flick of your wrist
       like a baseball pitcher.

It peels from your palm. It flies!
       It splats on a tree, on a wall.
Now throw it wherever you want.
       Throw it in the river.

The Hoopoe's Eye

Dusk. Suck-stepping over to the window,
a pistol shot explodes beneath my heel.
It's glass. A naked wall, empty of pictures;
there must be a picture lying here in wait.

Next day I dig it out. Uncovering the corner
of the frame I scrape off mud from glass. It's clear
the water's been inside, the mount is stained,
so I'm resigned; the picture's ruined.

Splinters of glass fan out like starshells
from the pressure point. I ease them out,
collect them for safety, only to meet the staring
of a hoopoe's eye, bright as the day it was painted,

brighter than ever I've seen it; the glazing,
muzzy haze of non-reflective glass –
I'd never realised - the medium is acrylic.
I wipe a trace of mud. The bird's unharmed.

Muddy Waters

They lie alone, face down in mud,
one by the drinks cupboard, the other
where the telephone should be.

Bridges are torn from soundboards,
the tension of the strings, cold water
has dissolved the luthier's glue.

They used to hang like siblings on the wall
ready to sing for every passer-by.
This old one's from East Germany, Keith's folly.

Bored stiff in Barrow, he fell for his teacher,
blunder-bust two marriages asunder.
Six quid I gave him, not the greatest

soundboard but a kindly action. The other
a bargain from the failing Music Shop,
a *liquidación*. That's funny now.

We used to finger-pick the blues; but one
has got a thunking tumour in its gut,
the other's ruptured. *Baby, please don't go.*

The Elephant in the Room

is not an elephant but a sturdy four-square table
still on its legs, but squint, offset from its station.
The William Morris table-cover's still in place,
and on its surface is a pale-wood fruit-bowl,
sycamore I think, which must have floated to the ceiling
settling back to its position as the tide went out.

So that's alright. Except if you try to shift it
all the legs fall off, they're loose. The tenons
have escaped, unglued, and now the sturdy table
stands unstable like a drunken elephant,
ready to slump into an elephant heap
if someone should unkindly give a shove.

The Olive Picks

On a shelf the mud lies thinner.
Stands to reason, for the water column
in a cupboard's shorter than it is outside.
But thick enough to hide things. Here's
an undecipherable object - a baby
carousel – you wipe the mud off,
recognise it, but the little picks
are missing, every one.

You work your fingers through the chill
of slippery clay, feeling for the points
like tiny tridents in a benthic ooze.
Here's one, and then a group of three,
and some have fallen to the floor
but when you wash them in the sink
the carousel is filled, with joy, complete.

Arbutus

In the north-east corner where the Strawberry Tree should be
and the Blackcap makes his presence felt each spring
now stands a scarecrow, tall and menacing
her figure scrawny, arms outstretched, her hair
struwelpeter'd into straw-pale bunches, and her waist
cinched-in with penitential briars, brambles, and her skirt
bedecked with twisted vinca bursting into flower
around her crinoline.

As in the fairytale I free her from barbarous lashings,
circling around her, snipping and tearing at prickles
and barbs, each garlanded with hanks of withered grass
and bunches of ripped-up roots and wild asparagus.
What I uncover is the armature the angry river raped,
the slender bones, the delicate ligatures intact.

I help her to her feet, steady her up with smelling salts
and foliar feed, and tie-in stakes to give her back support.

Treasure

Trowelling through mud, the blade
strikes timber. Nothing visible,
you scrape the surface layer clear
and find a cheap frame, bevels stapled.

No picture, just a slimy square
all wrinkled up. Recall a sunny day,
purchasing a set of four to mount
the lively decorated Suffolk tiles.

Like a blind mole you wedge through gloop.
Gloves hinder you. Peel off the Marigolds.
The edge is standing proud. Don't
prise it off the floor, you'll crack it.

Gently guddle, ease it out,
wipe clean the figure of a
sportive tropic fish, its tail
a flourish midst the sepia foliage.

Later we'll find the lizard tile,
its S-bend curling off
across the crusted mud.

Under the Sofa

Alarm call of milady, sharp,
head down under a capsized sofa.
Can't move fast, boots sucking,
feet sliding, heart pumping.
Bring a box she cries
it's a snake. I grab an empty
and there it is she has it cornered
steers it scoops it and it's
a sweetly-patterned chappie
big as a pinchos skewer
not much fatter, head swivelling
eyes blinking. I take the box
to the brink of the river
ask it politely to go away
say get out say scarper
and it does. In its own time.

Re-filling the Glass

Paco shows us with pride the water feature that he's built from stone
and mortar, carrying the little stream across his fresh-hosed garden.

He's smiling now, enthusiastic, though his house is ruined,
the chimney breast collapsed, the walls still sweating damp.

The salón floor is freshly-layed cement, Ricardo's mixing mortar
for the kitchen walls, and soon they'll lay it on, another task complete.

Lenguas de Gato*

I wonder shall I see once more the turtles
paddling up the re-configured Guadiaro,
hauling out like soup-plates on the unfamiliar rocks
to stew their bodies in the summer heat,
or hear the Cetti's warbler sing long afternoons
from his favourite cable, reinstated to the house.
The nightingale, I wonder will she nest again
in the papyrus by the terrace, or the flycatcher
knit and purl the air beneath the eaves.
Too soon the mare's tails thrust their spikes
competitive through mud and clay, racing the grasses
to the brilliant light of spring. The trees I think
will cope, or so I hope. But please remind me,
I must free the pear tree from its stranglement
garrotted in its flood-swept quince entanglement.
And will we feel again the passage of the Talgo train,
the early morning rumble of the Algeciras freight
boring its heavy passage from the docks.
I long to hear the kettle's gargled note,
the morning tea, the crumbling cat's tongue pastry
dissolving sugar-dusting in the throat.

*cat's tongues

Shutters

Shutters used to be bleached:
images of desiccated joinery
swinging listless in hot breezes
against the peeling ochre
of dismantled farmhouses.

Each framed panel was a foil
for strings of Spanish onions,
bentwood café chairs, and for the classic
waisted silhouette of blue guitars.

We used to do nostalgia, ennui, Camus
and the scent of casuarina
by the pine-fringed beaches:
also pinot grigio and langoustines.

But it's nearly half a century
and ennui's had its day. And I
am slathering the thirsty boards
with oil and thinners:
lifting the lustre in the grain
and giving second wind to shrivelled joints.

The Fly-Past

When you lie prone, your head
    in the shade of a fruiting almond,
your naked feet dangerously extended
    into the afternoon sunshine
and the flowering scent of the Persian Jewel Tree
    mingling in the heated air
with the *Hermès Calèche*
    of the lady beside you,
take heed of the sudden appearance above you
    of the king-sized carnivores,
their swift flight pausing
    as they enter a focussed spiral
and do them the honour of a salute
    with the right hand, fingers spread-eagled,
differentiating yourself from the corpse
    which you so vividly resemble
so they can immediately acknowledge
    your inherent vivacity with a flip
of their wingtips, and glide on
    down the valley in their regal search for a supper.

Feast Day

This is how it used to be, in all the brightness of a May morning
with the great pan up-ended against the olive tree
and the scraping and knocking clean, and I thought
a gilded hero would step forward with a maul to strike it
like a gong; but the focus was on cooking.

Then the pan was placed on three great stumps of wood,
thick and heavy to survive the day-long smouldering
and it was levelled by eye, logs and kindling thrust under
and fire set at several points, blown with a bellows;
and soon the ingredients appeared between the trees,
bins, boxes and buckets each capped with its cover,
and there were pans and jerry cans, and a select team
of cooks and under-cooks and the chief cook
who was the alcalde, the mayor, his neat grey beard,
his little round anarchist glasses.

First came the oil, glugged in from all sides,
pushed and spread about with three wooden paddles,
then big boxes of onions scalloped and shredded,
a little box of garlic squished and pulped
and boxes of chickens and turkeys that had walked
into something sharp and heavy; and the sizzling,
the frying and oil spitting filled the clearing with sound,
when a glittering flash passed over like an antique blessing,
not a sparrow but an oriole and it left
a shiver of gold in its wake.

The sub-cooks were signalled and the bags of rice
brought forward and slit and heaved in all round,
rice in kilos and kilos, and the oarsmen shoved
and sculled till it was oiled, translucent and glistening
and buckets of water were sloshed in as the anarchist
counted on his fingers, and soon the whole pan was slooshing
and the heat of the fire was intolerable and the water was roiling
and the anarchist brought forward a precious container,
peeled the lid off, revealing the liquor wherein the stamens
of a hundred thousand crocuses were steeping in their juices,
and he poured it with solemnity,
like a Libation to the Goddess.

The sun was high, and the people were gathering in their hunger,
in their keen anticipation: and there was a pause:
and the alcalde saw that it was good, and he gave the signal to the team
and they advanced with heavy rakes and pulled the fire from under,
pulling urgently the flaming logs, the smoking cinders and piling them
off to one side, where they could keep an eye on them, stamp out
the spreading flames if the grasses should ignite.

Then the women came forward with pails full of mussels, of cockles
of clams and razor shells, of scallops, crab of all sorts,
and in handfuls they tossed them across the seething mixture
(for the boiling continued long after the fire was extracted)
and the bubbling slowed, ceased, and on all sides the finishing touches
were being added, rosettes created from lettuces, tomatoes and peppers;
rosettes spread evenly around the perimeter.

Now every single cook looked happy and sweaty and confident,
and Julius stepped back and reached for a garland of rockets,
a handful of rockets, gripped in his fist, from his pocket he fished out
his ancient blue lighter and he held up the fireworks
just clear of his stubbly whiskers and he let them off swiftly
in a rapid-fire salvo and the percussion of firecrackers
echoed round the valley.

Then people came sauntering from their picnic rugs and cushions,
scattered round the amphitheatre, under the ancient olives,
approaching without haste the seven servers with their ladles
spaced round the circumference; and they fed a thousand people
on paper plates in less than ten minutes and by god it was good,
a paella to remember.

acknowledgement:
'Shutters' was first published in *Dream Catcher 28*

cover image:
detail from *Cosas de Formentera*, Betty Luton White, 1980

published by
Wayleave Press,
8 Buoymasters
St George's Quay,
Lancaster LA1 1HL
www.wayleavepress.co.uk

printed by
Andrew's, Main Street, Bentham LA2 7HQ